French Made Easy

Key Stage 2

AGES 7-11

Author and Consultant Charlotte Tomson

 Penguin Random House

Senior Editor Cécile Landau
Asst. Editor Nishtha Kapil
Art Editor Rashika Kachroo
Asst. Art Editor Kanika Kalra
Managing Art Editor Richard Czapnik
Pre-production Editor Francesca Wardell
French Consultant Charlotte Tomson
DTP Designer Anita Yadav
Dy. Managing Editor Soma B. Chowdhury

First published in Great Britain in 2014
This edition published in Great Britain in 2016
by Dorling Kindersley Limited
80 Strand, London, WC2R 0RL

Copyright ©2014, 2016 Dorling Kindersley Limited
A Penguin Random House Company

18 10 9 8 7 6 5 4 3 2
012–196495–07/16

A CIP catalogue record for this book
is available from the British Library
ISBN: 978-1-4093-4939-6

Printed and bound in China

All images © Dorling Kindersley Limited
For further information see: www.dkimages.com

A WORLD OF IDEAS:
SEE ALL THERE IS TO KNOW

www.dk.com

Contents

This chart lists all the topics in the book. Once you have completed each page, stick a star in the correct box below.

Page	Topic	Star
4	Bonjour! Comment tu t'appelles?	☆
5	Ça va?	☆
6	Les nombres 1–20	☆
7	Quel âge as-tu?	☆
8	Dans ma trousse	☆
9	Les adjectifs	☆
10	Les mois de l'année	☆
11	Quelle heure est-il?	☆

Say the following French phrases out loud.

Bonjour!
Hello!

Comment tu t'appelles?
What's your name?

Salut!
Hi!

Je m'appelle...
I'm/My name is...

Look at the pictures below. Then read out the pairs of greetings in the box on the left. Write the correct pair for each picture in the speech bubbles.

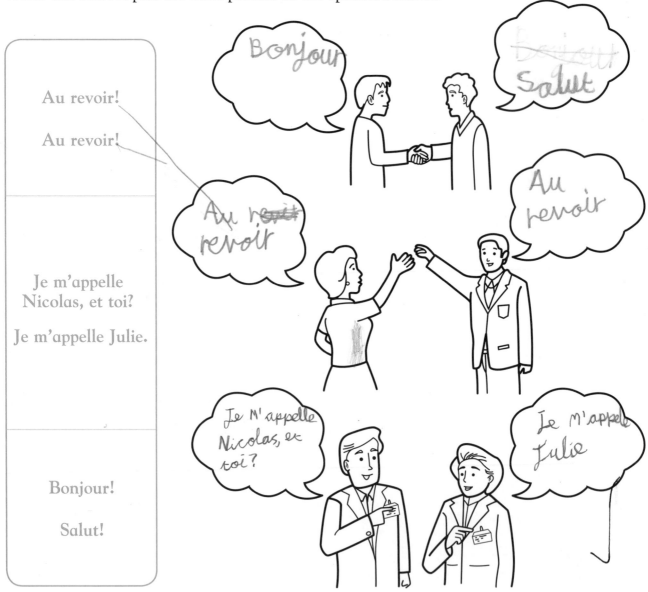

Here are two different ways of asking what someone's name is, but the vowels are missing. Can you supply them?

Comment t'appelles-tu?

Comment tu t'appelles?

> **Monsieur Hibou says, "When you ask a question in French, make your voice go up at the end. Practise with a friend."**

4

Look at these French expressions.

Ça va?	Pas mal!	Ça va bien, merci.	Ça ne va pas.
How are you?	Not bad!	I'm fine, thanks.	Not too well.

Now draw three faces in the box below: one happy and smiling, another looking sad and a third face that simply looks content and relaxed.

Choose an expression from above to match each of the faces you have drawn.

ça va bien, merci

Pas mal

ça ne va pas

Et toi? Ça va?

Monsieur Hibou says, "Watch out for French accents! The curly tail on the 'ç' is called a cedilla. It makes a soft 'c' instead of a hard 'c'. Also look out for 'â', 'é' and 'è' later in the book."

Les nombres 1-20

Point to each balloon and read the number on it out loud.

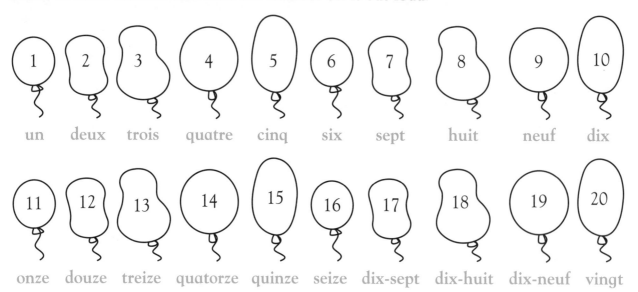

In the pictures below, numbers are shown in everyday situations.
Write the French word for each number shown below the pictures.

Monsieur Hibou says, "Keep revisiting numbers. Go for
a number walk. Every time you spot a number, say it in French."

Read these useful French sentences. Practise using them with family and friends, changing the number to match individual ages.

Quel âge as-tu?
How old are you?

J'ai dix ans.
I am ten.

J'ai cinq ans.
I am five.

J'ai seize ans.
I am sixteen.

Look at these pictures of people celebrating their birthdays.
Fill in the gaps in the speech bubbles.

The words in the sentences below have been mixed up. Rewrite the sentences with the words in the correct order.

1. six ans. J'ai   ....

2. ans. J'ai douze   ....

3. ai quatorze ans. J'   ....

4. J' dix-neuf ans. ai   ....

Monsieur Hibou says, "Remember to draw a little hat over the 'a' in âge. This accent (^) is called a circumflex."

Look at these pictures and read out the labels. Say what you have in your pencil case.

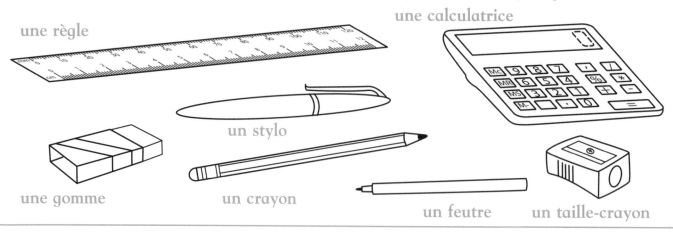

une règle

une calculatrice

un stylo

une gomme   un crayon   un feutre   un taille-crayon

These children are describing the contents of their pencil cases.
Read each description and match it to the correct group of objects shown below.

J'ai une gomme et deux crayons.

J'ai un stylo et une règle.

J'ai une calculatrice et trois feutres.

In French, all nouns (things or people) are either masculine or feminine.
The French word for *a* is either *un* or *une*, depending on whether the noun following it is masculine or feminine.

Put the words below in the correct place on the chart.

un stylo, une gomme, une règle, un crayon, un feutre, une calculatrice

Masculine	Feminine
....	....
....	....
....	....

Adjectives are used to describe people or things. Here are some useful French adjectives you may use to describe yourself or your friends.

| sympa | petit/petite | gourmand/gourmande |

| bavard/bavarde | paresseux/paresseuse | sportif/sportive |

Answer the following question. Use any adjectives you know, including those given above, in your reply.

| Tu es comment? | Je suis .... |
| What are you like? | I am .... |

Remember that adjectives in French 'agree' with the object or person they are describing. Fill in the missing words on the chart below.

English	Masculine Adjective	Feminine Adjective
....	sportif	....
....	....	paresseuse
talkative	....	....
small	....	....
....	....	gourmande
nice	....	....

Read out the list of months in the box on the right. Then look at the pictures below. Circle the month that best matches each picture.

			janvier février mars avril mai juin juillet août septembre octobre novembre décembre
novembre septembre	juin janvier	avril décembre	

février   juillet   octobre   mars   août   mai

Read these sentences.

Mon anniversaire, c'est le 4 juillet.
My birthday is on the 4th of July.

L'anniversaire de Sophie est le 8 février.
Sophie's birthday is on the 8th of February.

Now look at the notes from a Birthday Book on the left.
Use the information given to complete these sentences.

BIRTHDAYS

Julie 18th March   David 17th August
Thomas 4th June   Sam 10th May

L'anniversaire de Julie est ....

L'anniversaire de Thomas est ....

L'anniversaire de David est ....

L'anniversaire de Sam est ....

Et toi? C'est quand ton anniversaire?
And you? When is your birthday?

....

Monsieur Hibou says, "In French, months begin with a small letter, for example, *avril*. English uses a capital letter, for example, *April*."

Read out the times shown on the clock faces below.

 7:00   **7:15**   **11:30**   **8:45**

Il est sept heures.   Il est sept heures et quart.   Il est onze heures et demie.   Il est neuf heures moins le quart.

Read each sentence. Then circle the clock face above it showing that time.

Il est deux heures et demie.   Il est quatre heures moins le quart.   Il est six heures et quart.

 12:30   **02:00**   **09:45**   **08:45**   **01:30**   **01:00**

Il est deux heures.   Il est neuf heures moins le quart.   Il est une heure et demie.

Look at the phrases and pictures below.

| à midi | à onze heures | à cinq heures et quart | à minuit |
| at midday | at eleven o'clock | at quarter past five | at midnight |

Je me réveille.   Je me lave.   Je prends le petit déjeuner.   Je me brosse les dents.

Read the sentences below, describing regular morning activities. The times given are unusual. Rewrite each sentence, using times that match your morning routine.

Je me réveille à onze heures. ....

Je me lave à onze heures et demie. ....

Je prends le petit déjeuner à midi. ....

Je me brosse les dents à cinq heures et quart. ....

Here is a list of colours.

blanc	white	**jaune**	yellow	**marron**	dark brown
noir	black	**vert**	green	**brun**	brown
bleu	blue	**rose**	pink	**gris**	grey
rouge	red	**violet**	purple	**orange**	orange

Read the names of the colours out loud, then select from them to complete the sentences below.

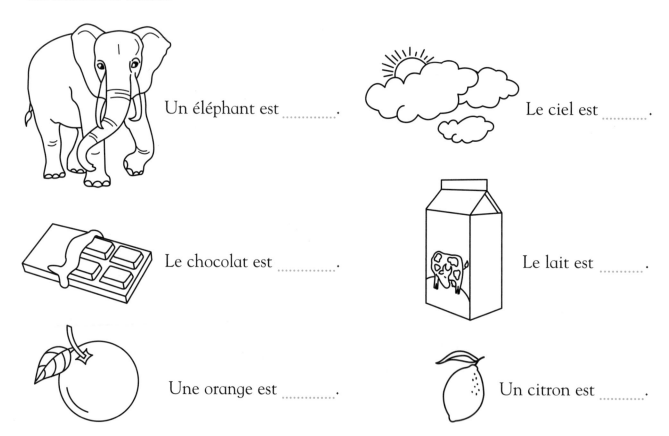

Un éléphant est ....

Le ciel est ....

Le chocolat est ....

Le lait est ....

Une orange est ....

Un citron est ....

Answer the following question.

Quelle est ta couleur préférée?   Ma couleur préférée est ....
What is your favourite colour?   My favourite colour is ....

Monsieur Hibou says, "Compare new French words with English words. Sometimes there are similarities which can help you remember them."

In French, colours go after the noun they describe. They must also be written in either their masculine or feminine form, depending on whether the noun is masculine or feminine.

un crayon bleu
a blue pencil

une gomme bleue
a blue rubber

Fill in the gaps to reveal the objects and their colours. You can look at pages 8 and 12 for any words you need.

1. A blue pen = u___ s_y___ bl_____

2. A blue ruler = un___ __è___ b_____

3. A black sharpener = u__ tai___-c_ay__ n__ n_____

4. A black rubber = un__ g__mm__ n_____

Draw lines linking the masculine and feminine forms of each colour listed.

Masculine	Feminine
marron	bleue
brun	jaune
bleu	marron
vert	rouge
rouge	rose
blanc	violette
jaune	brune
rose	verte
violet	blanche
gris	noire
noir	grise

Which colours stay the same? ....

Which colours needed more than 'e' adding to change from the masculine to feminine form? ....

Read the following words out loud. As you say each word, touch that part of your body.

le bras arm (plural: **les bras**)	**le pied** foot (plural: **les pieds**)	**la tête** head	
la jambe leg (plural: **les jambes**)	**l'oreille** ear (plural: **les oreilles**)	**la bouche** mouth	
le genou knee (plural: **les genoux**)	**la main** hand (plural: **les mains**)	**le ventre** tummy	
l'œil eye (plural: **les yeux**)	**l'épaule** shoulder (plural: **les épaules**)	**le nez** nose	

Use the words above to label the figure shown below.

Add 's' to an adjective, such as a colour, if you are using it to describe more than one thing.

Il a les yeux bleus.
He has blue eyes.

Il a les jambes longues.
He has long legs.

Read these sentences describing a monster. Circle the correct adjective to use in each case.

La tête est vert / verte.

Le ventre est gris / grise.

Il a les yeux jaunes / jaune.

Il a les jambes rouges / rouge.

La bouche est noir / noire.

Il a les oreilles grand / grandes.

Il a quatre bras bleu / bleus.

Now draw and colour the monster described.

Monsieur Hibou says, "Sssssh. When you add 's' to a plural, it is silent."

15

Read out the following French sentences and phrases.

Il a/Elle a les yeux bruns.
He has/She has brown eyes.

les yeux verts
green eyes

les yeux bleus
blue eyes

Il a/Elle a les cheveux blonds.
He has/She has blonde hair.

les cheveux noirs
black hair

Il a une barbe.
He has a beard.

Il porte/Elle porte des lunettes.
She wears glasses.

les cheveux courts
short hair

les cheveux longs
long hair

Now imagine you are the manager of a new pop band, *Les Trois Amis*.
Look at the picture below. Then use the words in the box under the picture
to fill in the gaps in the description of your band members.

Christelle   **Jean-Pierre**   **Sylvie**

barbe	longs	courts	et	lunettes
cheveux	Elle	a	yeux	

Christelle a les yeux bleus et les cheveux .... et blonds. Jean-Pierre a les ....
bruns et les .... courts et noirs. Il a une .... Sylvie .... les yeux verts
.... les cheveux marron et .... porte des ....

Read the following words and phrases.

mon père
my father

ma mère
my mother

Il/Elle s'appelle...
He/She is called...

Ils/Elles s'appellent...
They are called...

un frère
a brother

une sœur
a sister

Je n'ai ni frères, ni sœurs.
I don't have any brothers or sisters.

Je suis...
I am...

Il est...
He is...

Elle est...
She is...

Read this extract from a letter to a penpal. Then decide if the statements on the chart are true (*vrai*) or false (*faux*). Tick (✔) the right column. Look up any words you do not know in a dictionary or on the Internet.

Dans ma famille, il y a cinq personnes. Mon père s'appelle Jean-Pierre. Il est grand et marrant. Ma mère, Nicole, est petite et bavarde. J'ai deux soeurs qui s'appellent Sophie et Julie. Sophie a cinq ans et elle est timide. Julie a neuf ans. Elle a les cheveux blonds et longs. Elle est très paresseuse! Enfin, je m'appelle David. J'ai sept ans. J'ai les yeux verts et je porte des lunettes. Mon anniversaire est l'onze juillet. Je suis sportif et un peu gourmand! Et toi? As-tu des frères et des sœurs?

	Vrai	Faux
1. There are 4 people in the family.		
2. The father is called Jean-Pierre.		
3. The mother is talkative.		
4. David has a sister and a brother.		
5. Sophie is 9 years old.		
6. Julie has long blonde hair.		
7. Julie is shy.		
8. David is a bit greedy.		
9. David has blue eyes and wears glasses.		
10. David's birthday is on 11 July.		

Monsieur Hibou says, "There are three different ways of saying *my*. Use *mon* in front of a masculine noun, *ma* in front of a feminine noun and *mes* in front of a plural."

Look at the pictures of the different animals below. Read out the French word for each animal as you look at its picture.

un chien   un chat   un cheval

une souris   un oiseau   un lapin

Translate the English clues and complete the crossword puzzle.

Across

1. cat   ....

2. mouse   ....

3. horse   ....

Down

1. bird   ....

2. dog   ....

3. rabbit   ....

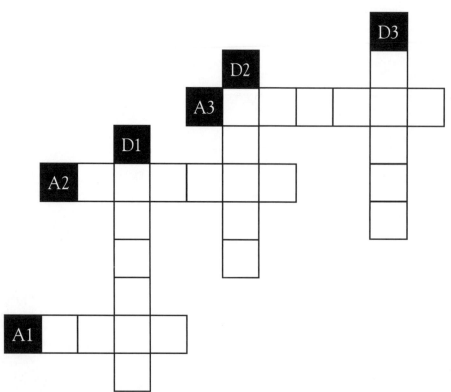

Most French plurals are formed by adding an 's' (which is silent).
But look out for these exceptions:

- words ending in 'al' change to 'aux'
- words ending in 'eau' change to 'eaux'
- words ending in 's' do not need another 's' added

Look at the French words illustrated below. Fill in the plural of each.

le serpent	l'oiseau	la souris	le cheval
les	les	les	les ....

Look at this key.

J'aime I like	☺	J'aime beaucoup I really like	☺ ☺
J'adore I love	☺ ☺ ☺	Je n'aime pas I don't like	⊗

Now use the key and the drawings below to build sentences.
The first one has been done for you.

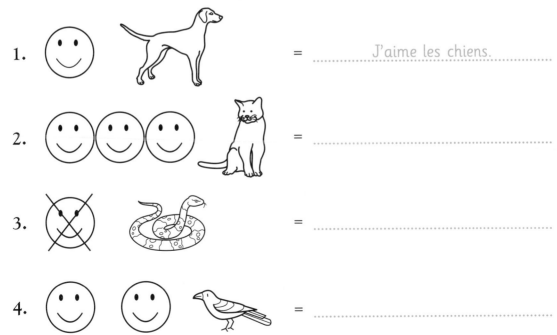

1.   ☺   🐕   = ... J'aime les chiens. ....

2.   ☺ ☺ ☺   🐈   = ...

3.   ⊗   🐍   = ...

4.   ☺ ☺   🐦   = ...

Look at the picture. The pets in this house are on the loose! Use the labels and position words in the box on the right to fill in the gaps in the description of the scene.

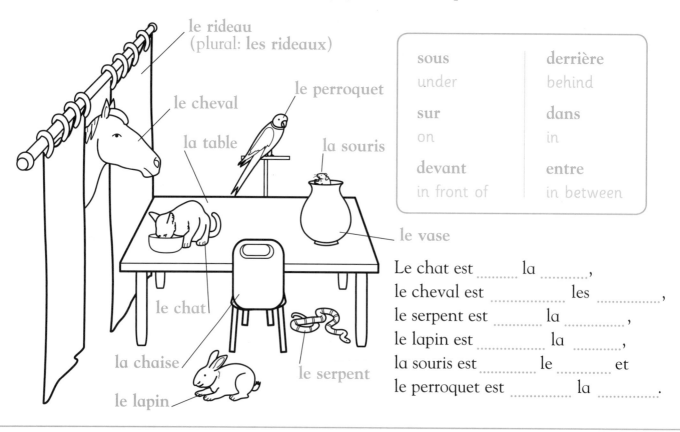

le rideau
(plural: les rideaux)

le perroquet

le cheval

la table

la souris

le vase

le chat

la chaise

le lapin

le serpent

sous	derrière
under	behind
sur	dans
on	in
devant	entre
in front of	in between

Le chat est .... la .... ,
le cheval est .... les .... ,
le serpent est .... la .... ,
le lapin est .... la .... ,
la souris est .... le .... et
le perroquet est .... la ....

Practise asking for and giving directions, using the map and sentences given below. Use a dictionary or the Internet to look up words you do not know.

Excusez-moi, où est la piscine?

Excuse me, where is the swimming pool?

Prenez la première rue à gauche/droite.

Take the first road on the left/right.

Prenez la deuxième rue à gauche/droite.

Take the second road on the left/right.

C'est à votre gauche/droite.

It is on your left/right.

Le cinéma

Le café

La boulangerie

Le musée

Le jardin public

La piscine

La gare

For example: "Excusez-moi, où est le musée?"
"Prenez la première rue à gauche.
C'est à votre droite."

Vous êtes ici
You are here

To make numbers over twenty, combine tens and units with a dash, just as you would in English. For example:

vingt-huit
twenty-eight

But watch out for the exception. When you add just one to the tens, you simply add *et un* (*and one*). For example:

vingt et un
twenty-one

Read out the numbers shown below.

vingt	trente	quarante	cinquante	soixante
20	30	40	50	60

Count the number of blocks and write the number in French below it.

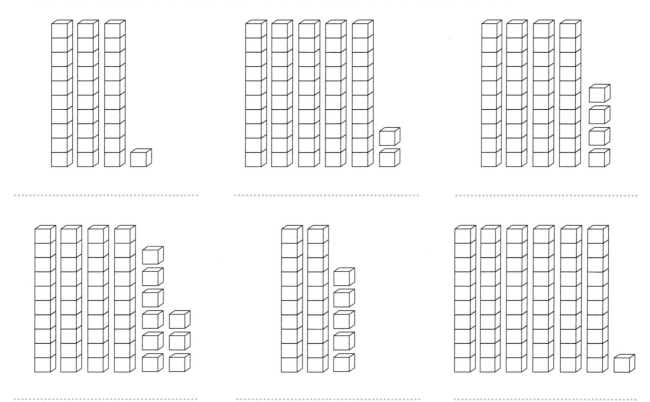

Write the answer to the following sums in French.

dix + vingt = ...

cinquante – quarante = ...

cinquante – dix = ...

quarante – vingt = ...

soixante + cinq = ...

quarante – cinq = ...

Monsieur Hibou says, "Keep practising numbers. Try counting backwards, counting in steps of two or clapping a rhythm."

Look at the key below. Read out the phrases describing the weather.

Il fait beau.
The weather is good.

Il fait chaud.
It is hot.

Il pleut.
It is raining.

Il y a des orages.
It is stormy.

Il fait mauvais.
The weather is bad.

Il fait froid.
It is cold.

Il y a du vent.
It is windy.

Il neige.
It is snowing.

Now use the map, key and compass points to complete
the weather report.

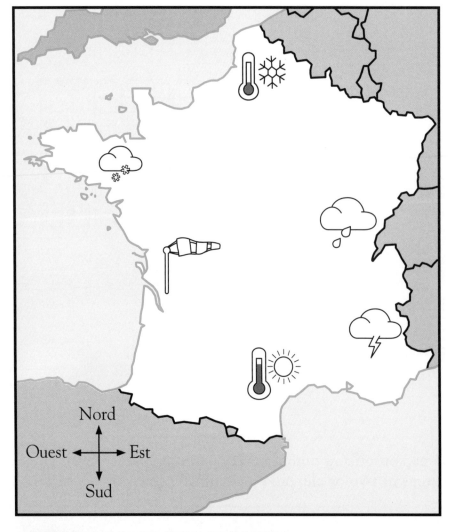

Voici la météo.
Here is the
weather report.

Dans le nord,
il fait froid. ....

Dans l'ouest,

....

Dans le nord-ouest,

....

Dans le sud,

....

Dans l'est,

....

Dan le sud-est,

....

Here are the days of the week in French. Read them out loud.

lundi	mardi	mercredi	jeudi
Monday	Tuesday	Wednesday	Thursday

vendredi	samedi	dimanche
Friday	Saturday	Sunday

Remember that the days of the week in French always start with a small letter.

Now read these sentences.

Quelle est la date aujourd'hui?   Aujourd'hui, c'est dimanche 15 août.
What is the date today?   Today, it is Sunday, 15th August.

Complete this sentence with today's date.

Aujourd'hui, c'est ....

Keep a weather diary for a week. Write a phrase to describe the weather for each day. For example:

Aujourd'hui, il fait beau.
Today, it is sunny.

lundi	mardi	mercredi	jeudi

vendredi	samedi	dimanche

Look at these sentences. Read them out loud. Adapt them to say which city, town or village you live in.

J'habite à Londres.
I live in London.

J'habite à Bristol.
I live in Bristol.

What kind of place do you live in? Is it big or small? Is it in town or in the country, by the sea or in the mountains? Use these sentences to describe it.

J'habite dans un village.
I live in a village.

J'habite dans une grande ville.
I live in a city.

J'habite dans une ville.
I live in a town.

J'habite en banlieue.
I live in the suburbs.

J'habite à la campagne.
I live in the country.

J'habite au bord de la mer.
I live by the sea.

J'habite à la montagne.
I live in the mountains.

Now translate these English sentences.

I live in Camden.   ....

I live in a town by the sea.   ....

I live in the country.   ....

I live in the suburbs.   ....

I live in a village in the mountains.   ....

Verbs are doing words. Many French verbs end with the letters 'er'. An example is habiter/to live. Pronounce 'er' as 'ay'. Study the chart below to see how verb endings change, depending on who the doer of the verb is.

J'	habite	I live
Tu	habites	You live
Il	habite	He lives
Elle	habite	She lives
Nous	habitons	We live
Vous	habitez	You live
Ils	habitent	They live
Elles	habitent	They live

Why do you think there are two ways of saying 'you live' and two ways of saying 'they live'?

....

....

....

....

....

....

Look at the phrases and pictures below.

dans un appartement
in an apartment

dans une maison
in a house

dans une ferme
on a farm

Build the sentences below to fit the pictures. Use the correct form of the verb 'habiter' and the phrases given on this page and page 24 opposite.

Nous habit ....

 Vous habit ....

Elles habit ....

★ La maison

Here are some of the rooms you will find in a house.

un salon	**une salle de bains**	**une cuisine**
a sitting room	a bathroom	a kitchen
une chambre d'enfants	**une salle à manger**	**une chambre**
a nursery	a dining room	a bedroom

au deuxième étage
on the second floor →

au premier étage
on the first floor →

au rez-de-chaussée
on the ground floor →

Imagine you are selling this house. Write a short description of what there is on each floor. Start by writing: **Au rez-de-chaussée, il y a...** / On the ground floor, there is...

....
....
....

Can you describe the rooms in your home? Start by writing:
Chez moi, il y a... / In my house, there is...

....
....
....
....

Here are the French words for various types of clothing.

un manteau	un pull	un jean
a coat	a jumper	some jeans
un chapeau	une écharpe	des gants
a hat	a scarf	some gloves
un tee-shirt	une jupe	une robe
a t-shirt	a skirt	a dress
des lunettes de soleil	des bottes	des chaussures
some sunglasses	some boots	some shoes

From the list above, pick out suitable clothes for the weather described in the following sentences. Use them to complete the sentences. For example:

Il fait froid. Je vais porter _un manteau et une écharpe._
It is cold. I am going to wear _a coat and a scarf._

Il neige. Je vais porter

Il fait chaud. Je vais porter

Il fait beau. Je vais porter

Tonight it is the school disco. Draw what you plan to wear. Describe your outfit. Start with:
Ce soir, je vais porter... / Tonight, I am going to wear...

Ce soir, je vais porter

Look at these activities. Can you work out from the pictures what they are in English?

jouer au foot

faire de l'équitation

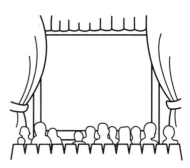

aller au cinéma

jouer à l'ordinateur

aller à la piscine

faire du vélo

Sophie is going on an activity holiday. Unscramble the activities (in brackets) in the programme below to plan her week. The first one has been done for you.

Lundi, ella va (al à nescipi) __à la piscine__ .

Mardi, ella va (ud refai ovél) _____ .

Mercredi, ella va (ed uttaqéioin l' rafie) _____ .

Jeudi, ella va (toof rejou ua) _____ .

Vendredi, ella va (ua éncima) _____ .

Et toi? Qu'est-ce que tu vas faire le weekend prochain ?
And you? What are you going to do next weekend?

Samedi, je vais _____ .

Dimanche, je vais _____ .

Use the phrases about activities to say what you like and do not like doing.

For example: **J'aime faire de l'équitation mais je n'aime pas jouer à l'ordinateur.**
           I like horse riding, but I do not like playing computer games.

J'aime _____ mais je n'aime pas _____ .

Look at the French words for the following numbers. Note how the words for 70, 80 and 90 are constructed.

70	80	90	100
soixante-dix	quatre-vingts	quatre-vingt-dix	cent
(60+10)	(4×20)	(4×20+10)	

Read out the numbers given below.

quatre-vingt-un   cent   quatre-vingt-dix

soixante-dix   soixante-douze   quatre-vingt-sept

quatre-vingt-trois   soixante-quinze   quatre-vingt-cinq

Do any of the numbers on the fish in the pond below match those given above? Colour them in.

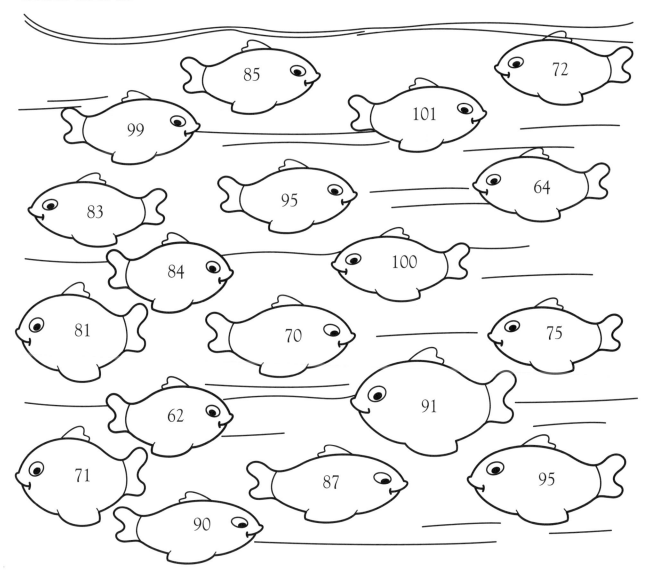

Bon appétit

Here is some of the food you may choose to take on a picnic.

un sandwich au jambon
a ham sandwich

du pain
some bread

un gâteau au chocolat
a chocolate cake

du fromage
some cheese

de la salade
some salad

une banane
a banana

une pomme
an apple

Look at each of the picnic plates below. Use the list of snacks given above to write about what you ate. Start with: **J'ai mangé...**   I ate...

J'ai mangé ....

....

J'ai mangé ....

....

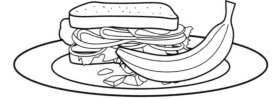

J'ai mangé ....

....

Read these two sentences.

Qu'est-ce que tu veux?
What would you like?

Je voudrais du pain s'il te plaît.
I would like some bread please.

Now imagine you are at a picnic. Say what you would like.

....

....

Monsieur Hibou says, "It is polite to say *s'il te plaît* **to a friend and** *s'il vous plaît* **when you are talking to someone you know less well."**

Here are some of the things you might order in a café or a restaurant.

une tranche de pizza	un jus d'orange	des frites	un coca
a slice of pizza	an orange juice	some chips	a cola

un sandwich au fromage | une glace à la fraise
a cheese sandwich | a strawberry ice cream

Look at the trays of food below. Then fill in the speech bubble for each order, matching what is on the tray. Start with: Je voudrais... / I would like...

Je voudrais
....
....

Je voudrais
....

Je voudrais
....
....

Read out this list of foods.

le riz	la viande	les carottes	l'eau
rice	meat	carrots	water
l'huile	les pâtes	le lait	la confiture
oil	pasta	milk	jam

At the supermarket, you have difficulty finding some of them and have to ask.

Vous avez...?   Je vais prendre...
Do you have...?   I'll have...

You will need to use the French words for 'some', which are:

du with a masculine noun   de la with a feminine noun
de l' with a noun starting with a vowel or silent 'h'   des with a plural noun

Now translate these sentences.

Do you have any milk? ....

I'll have some oil. ....

Do you have any carrots? ....

I'll have some meat. ....

Certificate

Congratulations to

....

for successfully finishing this book.

Ages
7-11

WELL DONE!

You're a star.

Date

....

Answer section with parents' notes

This book helps to support children's initial understanding of French. The exercises encourage children to take pleasure in and explore language. They also foster curiosity about the customs and culture of another country.

Contents

By working through the activities, your child will practise:
- saying his or her name and greeting people;
- expressing how he or she feels;
- counting from 1–100;
- asking people their age and saying his or her own;
- understanding the gender of nouns;
- describing nouns, using adjectival agreements;
- talking about times and dates, including birthdays;
- expressing preferences (about colours, pets and hobbies);
- describing simple appearances and clothes;
- understanding plural forms and the negative form;
- talking about position and directions;
- discussing the weather;
- understanding the conjugation of verbs;
- using the immediate future and the perfect tense;
- asking for things in shops and restaurants.

How to help your child

The activities in this book help children to express their thoughts in French and understand and respond to other people speaking French. Children need to practise new language in speaking and in writing. Encourage them to read their responses to exercises aloud, and practise asking questions as well as answering them. Help your child to explore meanings and spellings and to grasp basic language structures. Provide opportunities for further practice to help children begin memorising words and phrases. Also encourage the use of a dictionary to broaden their vocabulary. Have fun adapting words and structures seen here to create new sentences to use in everyday situations at home. Young children have a natural disposition for learning languages. Confidence in language at a young age will support future language learning.

Bon courage!

★ Bonjour! Comment tu t'appelles?

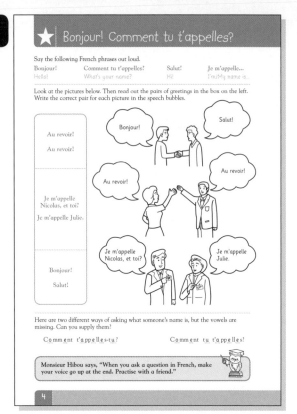

Say the following French phrases out loud.

Bonjour!	Comment tu t'appelles?	Salut!	Je m'appelle...
Hello!	What's your name?	Hi!	I'm/My name is...

Look at the pictures below. Then read out the pairs of greetings in the box on the left. Write the correct pair for each picture in the speech bubbles.

Au revoir!
Au revoir!

Je m'appelle Nicolas, et toi?
Je m'appelle Julie.

Bonjour!
Salut!

Bonjour!

Salut!

Au revoir!

Au revoir!

Je m'appelle Nicolas, et toi?

Je m'appelle Julie.

Here are two different ways of asking what someone's name is, but the vowels are missing. Can you supply them?

Comment t'appelles-tu?   Comment tu t'appelles?

Monsieur Hibou says, "When you ask a question in French, make your voice go up at the end. Practise with a friend."

Children should be able to greet each other with confidence. They should know the difference between *Salut!* and the more formal *Bonjour!*. Make sure that children have a chance to practise simple question forms too.

Ça va? ★

Look at these French expressions.

Ça va?	Pas mal!	Ça va bien, merci.	Ça ne va pas.
How are you?	Not bad!	I'm fine, thanks.	Not too well.

Now draw draw three faces in the box below: one happy and smiling, another looking sad and a third face that simply looks content and relaxed.
Choose an expression from above to match each of the faces you have drawn.

Ça va bien, merci.

Pas mal!

Ça ne va pas.

Et toi? Ça va?
Answers may vary

Monsieur Hibou says, "Watch out for French accents! The curly tail on the 'c' is called a cedilla. It makes a soft 'c' instead of a hard 'c'. Also look out for 'à', 'é' and 'è' later in the book."

Children should understand that when they ask a question, they need to raise their voice at the end. *Comment tu t'appelles?*, *Ça va?* and *Quel âge as-tu?* are ideal phrases for practising this skill.

★ Les nombres 1–20

Point to each balloon and read the number on it out loud.

1	2	3	4	5	6	7	8	9	10
un	deux	trois	quatre	cinq	six	sept	huit	neuf	dix

11	12	13	14	15	16	17	18	19	20
onze	douze	treize	quatorze	quinze	seize	dix-sept	dix-huit	dix-neuf	vingt

In the pictures below, numbers are shown in everyday situations. Write the French word for each number shown below the pictures.

Happy Birthday

quatre   quinze   dix-huit

treize   deux   dix

Monsieur Hibou says, "Keep revisiting numbers. Go for a number walk. Every time you spot a number, say it in French."

The numbers 1–16 require plenty of practice. Playing number games such as bingo will help. Children will find it useful to understand the pattern of numbers *dix-sept* (17), *dix-huit* (18) and *dix-neuf* (19) are similar to English 'teens'.

Quel âge as-tu? ★

Read these useful French sentences. Practise using them with family and friends, changing the number to match individual ages.

Quel âge as-tu?	J'ai dix ans.
How old are you?	I am ten.

J'ai cinq ans.	J'ai seize ans.
I am five.	I am sixteen.

Look at these pictures of people celebrating their birthdays. Fill in the gaps in the speech bubbles.

J'ai cinq ans.

J'ai trois ans.

J'ai huit ans.   J'ai seize ans.

The words in the sentences below have been mixed up. Rewrite the sentences with the words in the correct order.

1. six ans. J'ai   J'ai six ans.
2. ans. J'ai douze   J'ai douze ans.
3. ai quatorze ans. J'   J'ai quatorze ans.
4. J' dix-neuf ans. ai   J'ai dix-neuf ans.

Monsieur Hibou says, "Remember to draw a little hat over the 'a' in *âge*. This accent (^) is called a circumflex."

As well as replying to *Quel âge as-tu?*, children need to practise the question form so that they can initiate conversations themselves.

★ Dans ma trousse

Look at these pictures and read out the labels. Say what you have in your pencil case.

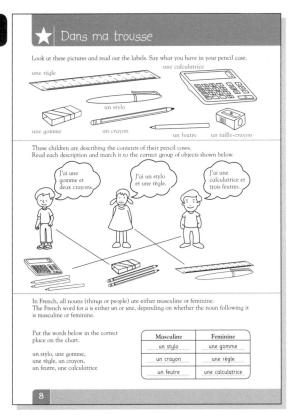

une règle
une calculatrice
un stylo
une gomme un crayon un feutre un taille-crayon

These children are describing the contents of their pencil cases.
Read each description and match it to the correct group of objects shown below.

J'ai une gomme et deux crayons.

J'ai un stylo et une règle.

J'ai une calculatrice et trois feutres.

In French, all nouns (things or people) are either masculine or feminine.
The French word for *a* is either *un* or *une*, depending on whether the noun following it is masculine or feminine.

Put the words below in the correct place on the chart.

un stylo, une gomme,
une règle, un crayon,
un feutre, une calculatrice

Masculine	Feminine
un stylo	une gomme
un crayon	une règle
un feutre	une calculatrice

This is the first collection of nouns and a useful opportunity for talking about the gender of nouns. Draw children's attention to *un* and *une* used for different nouns and compare against *a/an* in English.

Les adjectifs ★

Adjectives are used to describe people or things. Here are some useful French adjectives you may use to describe yourself or your friends.

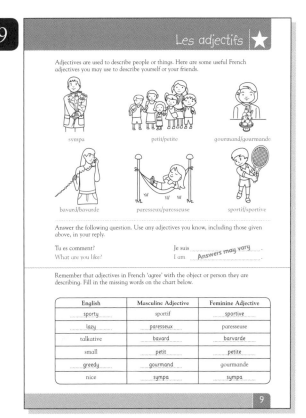

sympa petit/petite gourmand/gourmande

bavard/bavarde paresseux/paresseuse sportif/sportive

Answer the following question. Use any adjectives you know, including those given above, in your reply.

Tu es comment? Je suis _____ Answers may vary .
What are you like? I am _____ .

Remember that adjectives in French 'agree' with the object or person they are describing. Fill in the missing words on the chart below.

English	Masculine Adjective	Feminine Adjective
sporty	sportif	sportive
lazy	paresseux	paresseuse
talkative	bavard	barvarde
small	petit	petite
greedy	gourmand	gourmande
nice	sympa	sympa

Now that children know about gender, they can begin to use adjectives that agree with nouns. Point to the different spellings of masculine and feminine adjectives and ask children how the spelling has changed.

★ Les mois de l'année

Read out the list of months in the box on the right. Then look at the pictures below. Circle the month that best matches each picture.

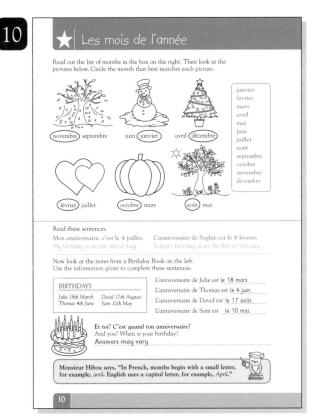

janvier
février
mars
avril
mai
juin
juillet
août
septembre
octobre
novembre
décembre

novembre septembre juin janvier avril décembre

février juillet octobre mars août mai

Read these sentences.
Mon anniversaire, c'est le 4 juillet. L'anniversaire de Sophie est le 8 février.
My birthday is on the 4th of July. Sophie's birthday is on the 8th of February.

Now look at the notes from a Birthday Book on the left.
Use the information given to complete these sentences.

BIRTHDAYS

Julie 18th March David 17th August
Thomas 4th June Sam 10th May

L'anniversaire de Julie est le 18 mars.
L'anniversaire de Thomas est le 4 juin.
L'anniversaire de David est le 17 août.
L'anniversaire de Sam est le 10 mai.

Et toi? C'est quand ton anniversaire?
And you? When is your birthday?
Answers may vary

Monsieur Hibou says, "In French, months begin with a small letter, for example, *avril*. English uses a capital letter, for example, *April*."

Children will enjoy talking about birthdays and saying more about themselves in French. They can begin by saying which month their birthday is in, e.g. *en janvier*, then progress to combining numbers and months.

Quelle heure est-il? ★

Read out the times shown on the clock faces below.

7:00 7:15 11:30 8:45

Il est sept heures. Il est sept heures et quart. Il est onze heures et demie. Il est neuf heures moins le quart.

Read each sentence. Then circle the clock face above it showing that time.

Il est deux heures et demie. Il est quatre heures moins le quart. Il est six heures et quart.

12:30 02:00 09:45 08:45 01:30 01:00

Il est deux heures. Il est neuf heures moins le quart. Il est une heure et demie.

Look at the phrases and pictures below.

à midi à onze heures à cinq heures et quart à minuit
at midday at eleven o'clock at quarter past five at midnight

Je me réveille. Je me lave. Je prends le petit déjeuner. Je me brosse les dents.

Read the sentences below, describing regular morning activities. The times given are unusual. Rewrite each sentence, using times that match your morning routine.
Je me réveille à onze heures.
Je me lave à onze heures et demie. Answers may vary
Je prends le petit déjeuner à midi.
Je me brosse les dents à cinq heures et quart.

It is a good idea to reinforce the numbers 1–12 before practising the time. Start by telling the time on the hour before progressing to half-hours and quarter-hours. Make sure children also practise the question form.

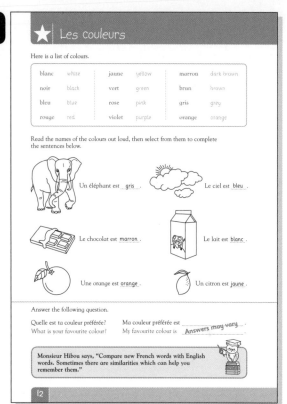

★ Les couleurs

Here is a list of colours.

blanc	white	jaune	yellow	marron	dark brown
noir	black	vert	green	brun	brown
bleu	blue	rose	pink	gris	grey
rouge	red	violet	purple	orange	orange

Read the names of the colours out loud, then select from them to complete the sentences below.

Un éléphant est _gris_ .

Le ciel est _bleu_ .

Le chocolat est _marron_ .

Le lait est _blanc_ .

Une orange est _orange_ .

Un citron est _jaune_ .

Answer the following question.

Quelle est ta couleur préférée? Ma couleur préférée est _____
What is your favourite colour? My favourite colour is _Answers may vary_ .

Monsieur Hibou says, "Compare new French words with English words. Sometimes there are similarities which can help you remember them."

12

Provide lots of opportunity to practise colours. It is a good idea to start with six colours and build from there. Children will enjoy listening to a colour sequence and repeating it.

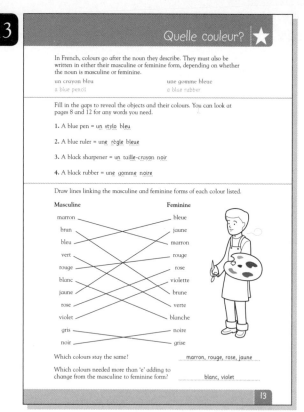

Quelle couleur? ★

In French, colours go after the noun they describe. They must also be written in either their masculine or feminine form, depending on whether the noun is masculine or feminine.

un crayon bleu une gomme bleue
a blue pencil a blue rubber

Fill in the gaps to reveal the objects and their colours. You can look at pages 8 and 12 for any words you need.

1. A blue pen = un stylo bleu

2. A blue ruler = une règle bleue

3. A black sharpener = un taille-crayon noir

4. A black rubber = une gomme noire

Draw lines linking the masculine and feminine forms of each colour listed.

Masculine	Feminine
marron	bleue
brun	jaune
bleu	marron
vert	rouge
rouge	rose
blanc	violette
jaune	brune
rose	verte
violet	blanche
gris	noire
noir	grise

Which colours stay the same? _marron, rouge, rose, jaune_

Which colours needed more an 'e' adding to change from the masculine to feminine form? _blanc, violet_

13

Colours are a good way of introducing children to adjectives following the noun. It would be useful to compare this page with page 9, which is also about adjectival agreement.

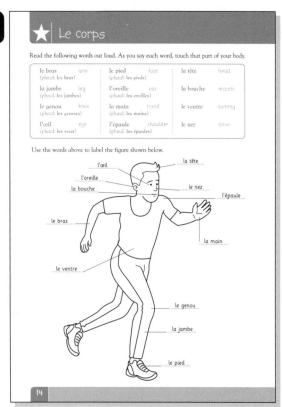

★ Le corps

Read the following words out loud. As you say each word, touch that part of your body.

le bras (plural: les bras)	arm	le pied (plural: les pieds)	foot	la tête	head
la jambe (plural: les jambes)	leg	l'oreille (plural: les oreilles)	ear	la bouche	mouth
le genou (plural: les genoux)	knee	la main (plural: les mains)	hand	le ventre	tummy
l'œil (plural: les yeux)	eye	l'épaule (plural: les épaules)	shoulder	le nez	nose

Use the words above to label the figure shown below.

l'œil
l'oreille
la bouche
la tête
le nez
l'épaule
le bras
la main
le ventre
le genou
la jambe
le pied

14

Point out to children the French for *the*: *le* (m.), *la* (f.), *l'* (before a vowel) and *les* (for a plural) used on this page.

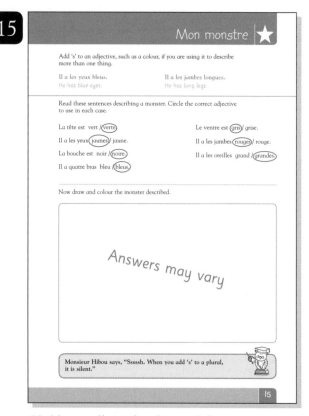

Mon monstre ★

Add 's' to an adjective, such as a colour, if you are using it to describe more than one thing.

Il a les yeux bleus. Il a les jambes longues.
He has blue eyes. He has long legs.

Read these sentences describing a monster. Circle the correct adjective to use in each case.

La tête est vert /(verte). Le ventre est (gris)/ grise.

Il a les yeux (jaunes)/ jaune. Il a les jambes (rouges)/ rouge.

La bouche est noir /(noire). Il a les oreilles grand /(grandes).

Il a quatre bras bleu /(bleus).

Now draw and colour the monster described.

Answers may vary

Monsieur Hibou says, "Sssssh. When you add 's' to a plural, it is silent."

15

Children will need to be confident using the verb *avoir*. Compare *J'ai* on page 7 with *Il a* on this page. Children here gain further practice at adjectival agreement.

★ Les portraits

Read out the following French sentences and phrases.

Il a/Elle a les yeux bruns.	les yeux verts	les yeux bleus
He has/She has brown eyes.	*green eyes*	*blue eyes*
Il a/Elle a les cheveux blonds.	les cheveux noirs	Il a une barbe.
He has/She has blonde hair.	*black hair*	*He has a beard.*
Il porte/Elle porte des lunettes.	les cheveux courts	les cheveux longs
She wears glasses.	*short hair*	*long hair*

Now imagine you are the manager of a new pop band, *Les Trois Amis*. Look at the picture below. Then use the words in the box under the picture to fill in the gaps in the description of your band members.

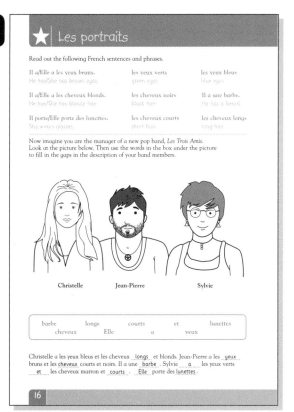

Christelle · Jean-Pierre · Sylvie

barbe	longs	courts	et	lunettes
cheveux	Elle	a	yeux	

Christelle a les yeux bleus et les cheveux __longs__ et blonds. Jean-Pierre a les __yeux__ bruns et les __cheveux__ courts et noirs. Il a une __barbe__. Sylvie __a__ les yeux verts __et__ les cheveux marron et __courts__. __Elle__ porte des __lunettes__.

Children will make progress by memorising set phrases. Here they again practise *avoir*, using both *Il a* and *Elle a*. Note that *marron* is an invariable adjective.

Ma famille ★

Read the following words and phrases.

mon père	ma mère	Il/Elle s'appelle...	Ils/Elles s'appellent...
my father	*my mother*	*He/She is called...*	*They are called...*
un frère	une sœur	Je n'ai ni frères, ni sœurs.	
a brother	*a sister*	*I don't have any brothers or sisters.*	
Je suis...	Il est...	Elle est...	
I am...	*He is...*	*She is...*	

Read this extract from a letter to a penpal. Then decide if the statements on the chart are true (*vrai*) or false (*faux*). Tick (✓) the right column. Look up any words you do not know in a dictionary or on the Internet.

Dans ma famille, il y a cinq personnes. Mon père s'appelle Jean-Pierre. Il est grand et marrant. Ma mère, Nicole, est petite et bavarde. J'ai deux sœurs qui s'appellent Sophie et Julie. Sophie a cinq ans et elle est timide. Julie a neuf ans. Elle a les cheveux blonds et longs. Elle est très paresseuse! Enfin, je m'appelle David. J'ai sept ans. J'ai les yeux verts et je porte des lunettes. Mon anniversaire est l'onze juillet. Je suis sportif et un peu gourmand! Et toi? As-tu des frères et des sœurs?

	Vrai	Faux
1. There are 4 people in the family.		✓
2. The father is called Jean-Pierre.	✓	
3. The mother is talkative.	✓	
4. David has a sister and a brother.		✓
5. Sophie is 9 years old.		✓
6. Julie has long blonde hair.	✓	
7. Julie is shy.		✓
8. David is a bit greedy.	✓	
9. David has blue eyes and wears glasses.		✓
10. David's birthday is on 11 July.	✓	

Monsieur Hibou says, "There are three different ways of saying *my*. Use *mon* in front of a masculine noun, *ma* in front of a feminine noun and *mes* in front of a plural."

Children need to be confident using the verb *être*. Compare *Je suis* against *Il est* and *Elle est*. The reading extract is a good exercise for children to use previous knowledge.

★ As-tu un animal?

Look at the pictures of the different animals below. Read out the French word for each animal as you look at its picture.

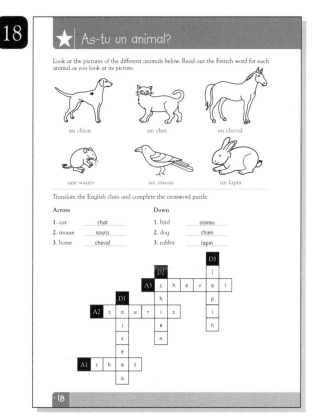

un chien · un chat · un cheval

une souris · un oiseau · un lapin

Translate the English clues and complete the crossword puzzle.

Across
1. cat __chat__
2. mouse __souris__
3. horse __cheval__

Down
1. bird __oiseau__
2. dog __chien__
3. rabbit __lapin__

Children gain further practice at *avoir*, here including the question form *As-tu un animal?*. Keep reminding children about the gender of nouns. Can children spot the feminine noun (*une souris*)?

Tu aimes les animaux? ★

Most French plurals are formed by adding an 's' (which is silent). But look out for these exceptions:
• words ending in 'al' change to 'aux'
• words ending in 'eau' change to 'eaux'
• words ending in 's' do not need another 's' added

Look at the French words illustrated below. Fill in the plural of each.

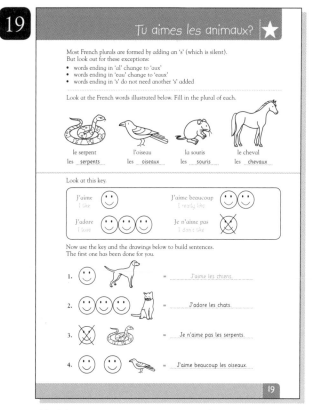

le serpent	l'oiseau	la souris	le cheval
les __serpents__	les __oiseaux__	les __souris__	les __chevaux__

Look at this key.

J'aime — *I like*	J'aime beaucoup — *I really like*
J'adore — *I love*	Je n'aime pas — *I don't like*

Now use the key and the drawings below to build sentences. The first one has been done for you.

1. = __J'aime les chiens.__
2. = __J'adore les chats.__
3. = __Je n'aime pas les serpents.__
4. = __J'aime beaucoup les oiseaux.__

Children enjoy expressing preferences. Here they are introduced to *J'aime* and the negative *Je n'aime pas*, which they could progress to applying to different contexts in the book, such as clothes and snacks.

Où est...?

Look at the picture. The pets in this house are on the loose! Use the labels and position words in the box on the right to fill in the gaps in the description of the scene.

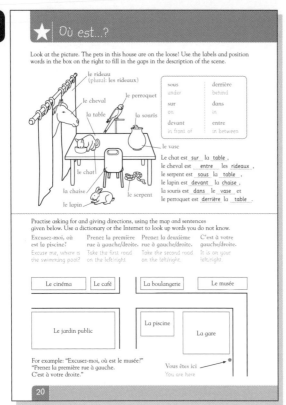

le rideau
(plural: les rideaux)

le cheval

le perroquet

la table

la souris

le vase

sous	derrière
under	behind
sur	dans
on	in
devant	entre
in front of	in between

le chat

la chaise

le lapin

le serpent

Le chat est _sur_ _la_ _table_ ,
le cheval est _entre_ les _rideaux_ ,
le serpent est _sous_ _la_ _table_ ,
le lapin est _devant_ _la_ _chaise_ ,
la souris est _dans_ _le_ _vase_ et
le perroquet est _derrière_ _la_ _table_ .

Practise asking for and giving directions, using the map and sentences given below. Use a dictionary or the Internet to look up words you do not know.

Excusez-moi, où est la piscine?
Excuse me, where is the swimming pool?

Prenez la première rue à gauche/droite.
Take the first road on the left/right.

Prenez la deuxième rue à gauche/droite.
Take the second road on the left/right.

C'est à votre gauche/droite.
It is on your left/right.

| Le cinéma | Le café | La boulangerie | Le musée |

| Le jardin public | La piscine | La gare |

For example: "Excusez-moi, où est le musée!"
"Prenez la première rue à gauche.
C'est à votre droite."

Vous êtes ici
You are here

Children practise *Excusez-moi* for politely asking questions. Encourage children to research additional vocabulary using a dictionary or the Internet. This a key skill in language learning.

Les nombres 20–60

To make numbers over twenty, combine tens and units with a dash, just as you would in English. For example:
vingt-huit
twenty-eight

But watch out for the exception. When you add just one to the tens, you simply add et un (and one). For example:
vingt et un
twenty-one

Read out the numbers shown below.

| vingt | trente | quarante | cinquante | soixante |
| 20 | 30 | 40 | 50 | 60 |

Count the number of blocks and write the number in French below it.

trente et un   cinquante-deux   quarante-quatre

quarante-neuf   vingt-cinq   soixante et un

Write the answer to the following sums in French.

dix + vingt = _trente_
cinquante – quarante = _dix_
cinquante – dix = _quarante_

quarante – vingt = _vingt_
soixante + cinq = _soixante-cinq_
quarante – cinq = _trente-cinq_

Monsieur Hibou says, "Keep practising numbers. Try counting backwards, counting in steps of two or clapping a rhythm."

For numbers such as 21 and 31, children need reminding to say *et* which helps with pronunciation. They can practise these higher numbers by talking about birthdays, counting everyday objects and playing games.

Quel temps fait-il?

Look at the key below. Read out the phrases describing the weather.

Il fait beau.
The weather is good.

Il fait chaud.
It is hot.

Il pleut.
It is raining.

Il y a des orages.
It is stormy.

Il fait mauvais.
The weather is bad.

Il fait froid.
It is cold.

Il y a du vent.
It is windy.

Il neige.
It is snowing.

Now use the map, key and compass points to complete the weather report.

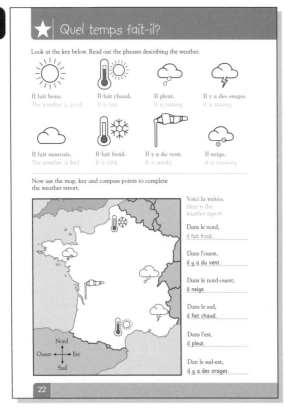

Voici la météo.
Here is the weather report.

Dans le nord,
il fait froid.

Dans l'ouest,
il y a du vent.

Dans le nord-ouest,
il neige.

Dans le sud,
il fait chaud.

Dans l'est,
il pleut.

Dan le sud-est,
il y a des orages.

Nord
Ouest — Est
Sud

Familiarise children with compass points by saying directions, while turning and pointing. Children should turn to face the same direction. Children will have fun creating their own weather maps and pretending to be weather presenters.

Les jours de la semaine

Here are the days of the week in French. Read them out loud.

| lundi | mardi | mercredi | jeudi |
| Monday | Tuesday | Wednesday | Thursday |

| vendredi | samedi | dimanche |
| Friday | Saturday | Sunday |

Remember that the days of the week in French always start with a small letter.

Now read these sentences.

Quelle est la date aujourd'hui?
What is the date today?

Aujourd'hui, c'est dimanche 15 août.
Today, it is Sunday, 15th August

Complete this sentence with today's date.

Aujourd'hui, c'est _Answers may vary_ .

Keep a weather diary for a week. Write a phrase to describe the weather for each day. For example:

Aujourd'hui, il fait beau.
Today, it is sunny

lundi	mardi	mercredi	jeudi
	Answers may vary		

vendredi	samedi	dimanche
	Answers may vary	

Try writing the days of the week on paper, jumbling and re-ordering them. Children can consolidate learning here by giving a full weather report, saying the day, date and weather for different regions.

★ Où habites-tu?

Look at these sentences. Read them out loud. Adapt them to say which city, town or village you live in.

J'habite à Londres.
I live in London.

J'habite à Bristol.
I live in Bristol.

What kind of place do you live in? Is it big or small? Is it in town or in the country, by the sea or in the mountains? Use these sentences to describe it.

J'habite dans un village.
I live in a village.

J'habite dans une grande ville.
I live in a city.

J'habite dans une ville.
I live in a town.

J'habite en banlieue.
I live in the suburbs.

J'habite à la campagne.
I live in the country.

J'habite au bord de la mer.
I live by the sea.

J'habite à la montagne.
I live in the mountains.

Now translate these English sentences.

I live in Camden.   *J'habite à Camden.*

I live in a town by the sea.   *J'habite dans une ville au bord de la mer.*

I live in the country.   *J'habite à la campagne.*

I live in the suburbs.   *J'habite en banlieue.*

I live in a village in the mountains.   *J'habite dans un village à la montagne.*

24

The phrases here will give children further opportunities to initiate conversation and say more about themselves. Point out the different ways here of saying *in*: à, dans and en.

Les verbes -er ★

Verbs are doing words. Many French verbs end with the letters 'er'. An example is habiter/to live. Pronounce 'er' as 'ay'. Study the chart below to see how verb endings change, depending on who the doer of the verb is.

J'	habite	I live
Tu	habites	You live
Il	habite	He lives
Elle	habite	She lives
Nous	habitons	We live
Vous	habitez	You live
Ils	habitent	They live
Elles	habitent	They live

Why do you think there are two ways of saying 'you live' and two ways of saying 'they live'?

'Tu' is singular and 'vous' is plural. But 'vous' is also more formal than 'tu'; 'vous' is used for someone (singular) you don't know very well; 'tu' is for friends and family. 'Ils' is masculine and 'Elles' is feminine, but for a mixed group, you also use 'Ils'.

Look at the phrases and pictures below.

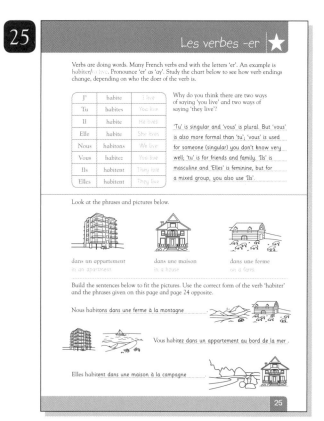

dans un appartement
in an apartment

dans une maison
in a house

dans une ferme
on a farm

Build the sentences below to fit the pictures. Use the correct form of the verb 'habiter' and the phrases given on this page and page 24 opposite.

Nous habitons dans une ferme à la montagne

Vous habitez dans un appartement au bord de la mer.

Elles habitent dans une maison à la campagne

25

Children are introduced to the present tense of a regular -er verb. The different forms are very different to English. Ask children which letters have been added to *habit* for each form (*je, tu, il* etc.).

★ La maison

Here are some of the rooms you will find in a house.

un salon
a sitting room

une salle de bains
a bathroom

une cuisine
a kitchen

une chambre d'enfants
a nursery

une salle à manger
a dining room

une chambre
a bedroom

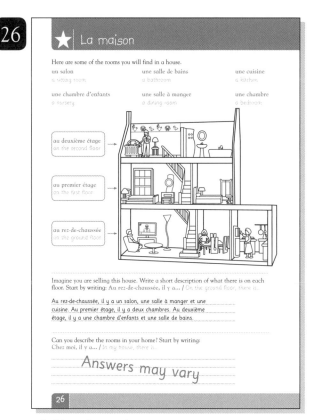

au deuxième étage
on the second floor

au premier étage
on the first floor

au rez-de-chaussée
on the ground floor

Imagine you are selling this house. Write a short description of what there is on each floor. Start by writing: Au rez-de-chaussée, il y a... / On the ground floor, there is...

Au rez-de-chaussée, il y a un salon, une salle à manger et une cuisine. Au premier étage, il y a deux chambres. Au deuxième étage, il y a une chambre d'enfants et une salle de bains.

Can you describe the rooms in your home? Start by writing: Chez moi, il y a... / In my house, there is...

Answers may vary

26

Children have the opportunity to write a short text of their own and practise the words *il y a* (there is/there are) and *et* (and). Children could revise numbers and plurals here too.

Les vêtements ★

Here are the French words for various types of clothing.

un manteau
a coat

un pull
a jumper

un jean
some jeans

un chapeau
a hat

une écharpe
a scarf

des gants
some gloves

un tee-shirt
a t-shirt

une jupe
a skirt

une robe
a dress

des lunettes de soleil
some sunglasses

des bottes
some boots

des chaussures
some shoes

From the list above, pick out suitable clothes for the weather described in the following sentences. Use them to complete the sentences. For example:

Il fait froid. Je vais porter   *un manteau et une écharpe.*
It is cold. I am going to wear   *a coat and a scarf.*

Il neige. Je vais porter
Answers may vary

Il fait chaud. Je vais porter
Answers may vary

Il fait beau. Je vais porter
Answers may vary

Tonight it is the school disco. Draw what you plan to wear. Describe your outfit. Start with:
Ce soir, je vais porter... / Tonight, I am going to wear:

Answers may vary

Ce soir, je vais porter

Answers may vary

27

Point out the use of *des* (some), used with plural nouns. Children are also introduced to the immediate future tense – *je vais* + an infinitive verb. They will enjoy using known structures here in new contexts.

Les passe-temps

Look at these activities. Can you work out from the pictures what they are in English?

jouer au foot   faire de l'équitation   aller au cinéma

jouer à l'ordinateur   aller à la piscine   faire du vélo

Sophie is going on an activity holiday. Unscramble the activities (in brackets) in the programme below to plan her week. The first one has been done for you.

Lundi, ella va (al à nescipi) __à la piscine__ .

Mardi, ella va (ud refai ovél) __faire du vélo__ .

Mercredi, ella va (ed uttaqéioin l' rafie) __faire de l'équitation__ .

Jeudi, ella va (toof rejou ua) __jouer au foot__ .

Vendredi, ella va (ua éncima) __au cinéma__ .

Et toi? Qu'est-ce que tu vas faire le weekend prochain ?
And you? What are you going to do next weekend?

Samedi, je vais _____ **Answers may vary** _____ .

Dimanche, je vais _____ **Answers may vary** _____ .

Use the phrases about activities to say what you like and do not like doing.

For example: J'aime faire de l'équitation mais je n'aime pas jouer à l'ordinateur.
I like horse riding, but I do not like playing computer games.

J'aime **Answers may vary** mais je n'aime pas **Answers may vary** .

Here children practise further forms of the immediate future tense, for example *Elle va faire*. Point out that *On Monday* translates as just *Lundi*. The connective *mais* will allow children to extend their sentences.

Les nombres 70-100

Look at the French words for the following numbers. Note how the words for 70, 80 and 90 are constructed.

70	80	90	100
soixante-dix	quatre-vingts	quatre-vingt-dix	cent
(60+10)	(4×20)	(4×20+10)	

Read out the numbers given below.

quatre-vingt-un	cent	quatre-vingt-dix
soixante-dix	soixante-douze	quatre-vingt-sept
quatre-vingt-trois	soixante-quinze	quatre-vingt-cinq

Do any of the numbers on the fish in the pond below match those given above? Colour them in.

To learn these higher numbers, children need to combine numbers they have already seen on pages 6 and 21. Children could practise by taking measurements and talking about money (euros and cents).

Bon appétit

Here is some of the food you may choose to take on a picnic.

un sandwich au jambon	du pain	un gâteau au chocolat
a ham sandwich	some bread	a chocolate cake
du fromage	de la salade	une banane	une pomme
some cheese	some salad	a banana	an apple

Look at each of the picnic plates below. Use the list of snacks given above to write about what you ate. Start with: J'ai mangé... I ate...

J'ai mangé du pain, de la salade et une pomme .

J'ai mangé un sandwich au jambon et une banane .

J'ai mangé du fromage et un gâteau au chocolat .

Read these two sentences.

Qu'est-ce que tu veux?   Je voudrais du pain s'il te plaît.
What would you like?   I would like some bread please.

Now imagine you are at a picnic. Say what you would like.

Answers may vary

Monsieur Hibou says, "It is polite to say *s'il te plaît* to a friend and *s'il vous plaît* when you are talking to someone you know less well."

Children can practise these phrases at the table. They are introduced to the perfect tense of a regular -er verb: *j'ai mangé*. They also have further practice speaking in a polite way (see page 20).

Que désirez-vous?

Here are some of the things you might order in a café or a restaurant.

une tranche de pizza	un jus d'orange	des frites	un coca
a slice of pizza	an orange juice	some chips	a cola
un sandwich au fromage		une glace à la fraise	
a cheese sandwich		a strawberry ice cream	

Look at the trays of food below. Then fill in the speech bubble for each order, matching what is on the tray. Start with: Je voudrais... / I would like...

Je voudrais une tranche de pizza et un jus d'orange

Je voudrais des frites et un coca

Je voudrais un sandwich au fromage et une glace à la fraise

Read out this list of foods.

le riz	la viande	les carottes	l'eau
rice	meat	carrots	water
l'huile	les pâtes	le lait	la confiture
oil	pasta	milk	jam

At the supermarket, you have difficulty finding some of them and have to ask.

Vous avez...?   Je vais prendre...
Do you have...?   I'll have...

You will need to use the French words for 'some', which are:
du with a masculine noun   de la with a feminine noun
de l' with a noun starting with a vowel or silent 'h'   des with a plural noun

Now translate these sentences.

Do you have any milk? __Vous avez du lait?__

I'll have some oil. __Je vais prendre de l'huile.__

Do you have any carrots? __Vous avez des carrottes?__

I'll have some meat. __Je vais prendre de la viande.__

Encourage children to use the structures provided (*Je vais prendre* and *Vous avez...?*) and work their way through the whole list of foods for further reinforcement of *du, de la, de l'* and *des*.